I0210558

William Strode

Shearsman Classics Vol. 5

Other titles in the *Shearsman Classics* series:

1. *Poets of Devon and Cornwall, from Barclay to Coleridge*
(ed. Tony Frazer)
2. Robert Herrick: *Selected Poems* (ed. Tony Frazer)
3. *Spanish Poetry of the Golden Age,*
in contemporary English translations (ed. Tony Frazer)
4. Mary, Lady Chudleigh: *Selected Poems* (ed. Julie Sampson)

Selected Poems

of

William Strode

Selected & edited by
Tony Frazer

Shearsman Books
Exeter

First published in the United Kingdom in 2009 by
Shearsman Books Ltd
58 Velwell Road
Exeter EX4 4LD

www.shearsman.com

ISBN 978-1-84861-005-7
First Edition

Notes and editorial matter
copyright © Shearsman Books Ltd, 2009.

Contents

Introduction   8

Lyrics
Song: "When Orpheus sweetly did complayne"   11
Song: In commendation of Musick   12
Song: "Keepe on your maske"   13
Another version   14
Song: "O when will Cupid shew such arte"   15
Song: On a Sigh   16
Song: On the Baths   18
Song: "As I out of a casement sent"   20
Song: On a Friend's Absence   22
Song: Melancholly   23
Song: Opposite to Melancholly   24

A Translation of the Nightingale out of Strada   25

Miscellaneous Poems
On Westwell Downes   28
On a great hollow Tree   30
On Fayrford Windowes   33
On a Gentlewoman's blistred lipp   36
To a Gentlewoman for a Friend   37
For a Gentleman, who, kissing his Friend at his
    departure, left a sign of blood on her   39
On a Dissembler   40
On Gray Eyes   41
On a Gentlewoman's Watch that wanted a key   43
A Watch sent home to Mrs. Eliz. King   44
On a watch made by a Blacksmith   44
On a Gentlewoman that sung and play'd upon a Lute   45
Upon the blush of a faire Ladie   45
On a Gentlewoman walking in the Snowe   46
On Chloris standing by the Fire   46
To a Valentine   47

A Superscription on Sir Philip Sidney's Arcadia   47
On the Picture of two Dolphins in a Fountayne   48
Sonnet: "My love and I for kisses play'd"   48
To his Mistress " In your sterne beauty I can see"   49
A Lover to his Mistress   49
A Riddle: on a Kiss   50
On a Gentlewoman that had had the small poxe   50
On Jealousy   51

Religious Poems
Of Death & Resurrection   52
On the Bible   53
On a Register for the Bible   54
Anthem for Good Fryday   54
An Antheme   55
Justification   55
On the Life of Man   56

Elegies
On the death of of Mrs. Mary Neudham   56
On the Death of Mistress Mary Prideaux   57
On the same M. M. P.   58
Consolatorium, Ad Parentes   59
Her Epitaph   60
On the Death of Sir Tho. Peltham   62
On the Death of a Twin   63
On the yong Baronett Portman   64
On the Death of Dr. Lancton   66
On the Death of Sir Thomas Lea   68
An Epitaph on Sr. John Walter   70
On the death of Sir Rowland Cotton . . .   71
To the Right Honourable the Lady Penelope,
     Dowager of the late Viscount Bayning   72
On the death of the Right Hon. the Lord Viscount Bayning 73
On the Death of the Ladie Caesar   75
An Epitaph on Mr. Fishborne   77
On the Death of Mr. James Van Otton   80

| On Sir Thomas Savill dying of the small pox | 81 |
| Epitaph on Mr. Bridgman | 81 |

Epistles

To his Sister	82
A New Year's Gift	83
To a Friend	84
A Letter	85
With Penne, Inke, and Paper to a distressed Friend	86
Thanks for a Welcome	86

Humorous Poems

A Paralell between Bowling and Preferment	87
On a good legg and foot	88
On John Dawson (Butler of C.C.)	89
Jacke-on-both-sides	90
The Chimney-Sweeper's Song	91
Upon the Sheriffs Beere	93
On a butcher Marrying a Tanner's Daughter	93
A Devonshire Song	95
Love compared to a game of tables	95
Epitaphes on the Monument of Sir William Strode	96

Poems of Uncertain Attribution

A Sonnet: "Mourne, mourne, yee lovers"	97
A Sonnet: "Sing aloud, harmonious sphears"	97
On his Mistresse	98
Upon a Gentlewoman's Entertainment of Him	99

| Notes | 102 |

Introduction

The casual reader's first response on seeing a volume of William Strode's poems is more than likely to be: "Who's that?", for William Strode is an almost forgotten figure, except with those readers who pay careful attention to compendious anthologies of Jacobean and Caroline verse, where Strode is often represented by a poem or two. Anyone who had been interested by those few anthologised gems would have drawn a blank when looking for more of the poet's work, because there has only ever been a single volume of his work, edited and published by the indefatigable Bertram Dobell, in London in 1907. I found a copy of this through the antiquarian book trade and it was instructive that the copy—at that point 99 years old—still had uncut pages. Having read the book, I came to the conclusion that Strode little deserved his oblivion. He is not a major poet, but nor should he be ignored. At a time when England was blessed with a large number of first-rank poets, a secondary figure such as Strode is easily forgotten, obscured by the shade cast by mightier figures. For readers in the West Country, in particular, Strode, a native of Devon, should be part of their heritage—although it must be admitted that his work has more to do with Oxford and London than it has with Devon, with the exception of the dialect poem, 'A Devonshire Song'.

Strode did not go quite unpublished, however: his play, *The Floating Island*, was printed in London in 1655, but seems to have had little impact. The play itself, written for the visit of Charles II to Oxford, also appears to have had minimal impact in performance—although some recorded comments from its single performance suggest that it was not regarded as an *exciting* occasion. Strode's poems, however, turned up frequently in commonplace books of the era and in printed miscellanies—indications that his work was held in some esteem by his contemporaries.

William Strode was born in the county of Devon in either 1600 or 1601, in the parish of Plympton St. Mary—then a separate township, but today subsumed within the boundaries of Plympton, itself now a township on the very edge of greater Plymouth. His father was one Philip Strode, and William appears to have been the only son, although the address of one of his poems indicates that he had at least one sister. A successful and diligent scholar, Strode went up to Christ Church College, Oxford from Westminster School, probably in 1617, and there took his first degree in 1621. He became Master of Arts in 1624, after which he entered the Church, becoming a preacher with the University. In 1629 he was awarded the post of Proctor and also Public Orator, the latter no doubt a tribute to his verbal powers. In 1631, he was awarded the degree of Bachelor of Divinity. It seems he was to stay in Oxford for the rest of his days. From 1628 to 1635 he also served as Chaplain to the Bishop of Oxford, a post which would have brought him additional income, and in 1633 he became Rector of East Bradenham in Norfolk, although it would appear that he did not leave Oxford—he no doubt appointed a Chaplain to manage the living. From 1639 to 1642 he was Vicar of Badley, Northants, no doubt in a similar manner. Strode was married and had one daughter, but was to die in 1645 in Oxford, and was buried in Christ Church Cathedral.

Such are the bare bones of Strode's life, and precious little more is to be had. We do have his poems, however. I have selected almost all of his lyric poems (leaving out only the minor 'Posies'), as well as a large number of his elegies, although I elected against a more thorough survey of the latter, given the somewhat repetitive nature of these tribute poems. No selection has been made from *The Floating Island*, which seems to belong in another kind of book entirely.

Tony Frazer
Exeter, 2009

Song

When Orpheus sweetly did complayne
Upon his lute with heavy strayne
How his Eurydice was slayne,
    The trees to heare
    Obtayn'd an eare,
And after left it off againe.

At every stroake and every stay
The boughs kept time, and nodding lay,
And listened bending all one way:
    The aspen tree
    As well as hee
Began to shake and learn'd to play.

If wood could speak, a tree might heare,
If wood could sound true greife so neare
A tree might dropp an amber teare:
    If wood so well
    Could ring a knell
The Cipres might condole the beare.

The standing nobles of the grove
Hearing dead wood so speak and move
The fatall axe beganne to love:
    They envyde death
    That gave such breath
As men alive doe saints above.

Song: In commendation of Musick

When whispering straynes doe softly steale
With creeping passion through the hart,
And when at every touch wee feele
Our pulses beate and beare a part;
    When thredds can make
    A hartstring shake
    Philosophie
    Can scarce deny
The soule consists of harmony.

When unto heavenly joy wee feyne
Whatere the soule affecteth most,
Which onely thus wee can explayne
By musick of the winged host,
    Whose layes wee think
    Make starres to winke,
    Philosophie
    Can scarce deny
Our soules consist of harmony.

O lull mee, lull mee, charming ayre,
My senses rock with wonder sweete;
Like snowe on wooll thy fallings are,
Soft, like a spiritts, are thy feete:
    Greife who need feare
    That hath an eare?
    Down lett him lye
    And slumbring dye,
And change his soule for harmony.

SONG

Keepe on your maske, and hide your eye,
For with beholding you I dye:
Your fatall beauty, Gorgon-like,
Dead with astonishment will strike;
Your piercing eyes if them I see
Are worse than basilisks to mee.

Shutt from mine eyes those hills of snowe,
Their melting valleys doe not showe;
Their azure paths lead to dispaire,
O vex me not, forbeare, forbeare;
For while I thus in torments dwell
The sight of heaven is worse than hell.

Your dayntie voice and warbling breath
Sound like a sentence pass'd for death;
Your dangling tresses are become
Like instruments of finall doome.
O if an Angell torture so,
When life is done where shall I goe?

ANOTHER VERSION, TO HIS MISTRESSE

Keepe on your mask and hide your eye
For in beholding you I dye.
Your fatall beauty Gorgon-like
Dead with astonishment doth strike.
Your piercing eyes that now I see
Are worse than Basilisks to me.
Shut from mine eyes those hills of snow,
Their melting vally do not shew:
Those azure paths lead to despaire,
O vex me not, forbear, forbear;
For while I thus in torments dwell
The sight of Heaven is worse than Hell.
In those faire cheeks two pits doe lye
To bury those slaine by your eye:
So this at length doth comfort me
That fairely buried I shall be:
My grave with Roses, Lillies, spread,
Methinks tis life for to be dead:
Come then and kill me with your eye,
For if you let me live I dye.
     When I perceive your lips againe
Recover those your eyes have slaine,
With kisses that (like balsome pure)
Deep wounds as soon as made doe cure,
Methinks tis sicknesse to be sound,
And there's no health to such a wound.
When in your bosome I behold
Two hills of snow yet never cold,
Which lovers, whom your beauty kills,
Revive by climing those your hills,
Methinks there's life in such a death
That gives a hope of sweeter breath:
Then since one death prevails not where

So many antidotes are nere,
And your bright eyes doe but in vain
Kill those who live as fast as slaine;
That I no more such death survive
Your way's to bury me alive
In place unknown, and so that I
Being dead may live and living dye.

Song

O when will Cupid shew such arte
To strike two lovers with one darte?
I'm ice to him or hee to mee;
Two hearts alike there seldome bee.

If thrice ten thousand meete together
How scarce one face is like another!
If scarce two faces can agree
Two hearts alike there seldome bee.

SONG: ON A SIGH

O tell mee, tell, thou god of wynde,
In all thy cavernes canst thou finde
A vapour, fume, a gale or blast
Like to a sigh which love doth cast?
Can any whirlwynde in thy vault
Plough upp earth's breast with like assault?
    Goe wynde and blow thou where thou please,
    Yea breathles leave mee to my ease.

If thou be wynde, O then refrayne
From wracking whiles I thus complayne:
If thou be wynde then light thou art,
Yet O! how heavy is my hart!
If thou be wynde then purge thy way,
Lett cares that clogge thy force obey.
    Goe wynde and blowe thou where thou please,
    Yea breathles leave mee to my ease.

Those blasts of sighing raised are
By influence of my bright starre;
Their Æolus from whom they came
Is love that straynes to blow his flame,
The powerfull sway of whose behest
Makes hearth and bellowes of my breast.
    Goe wynde and blow then where thou please,
    Yea breathles leave mee to my ease.

Know 'tis a wynde that longs to blowe
Upon my Saint wherere shee go,
And stealing through her fanne it beares
Soft errands to her lippes and eares,
And then perhapps a passage makes
Downe to her heart when breath shee takes.

Goe wynde and blowe then where thou please,
Yea breathles leave mee to my ease.

Yes, gentle gale, trye that againe,
O doe not passe from mee in vayne,
Goe mingle with her soul divine
Ingendring spiritts like to mine:
Yea take my soule along with thee
To worke a stronger sympathie:
    Go wynde and blowe thou where thou please,
    Yea breathles leave mee to my ease.

My soule, before my grosser part,
Thus to her heaven should departe,
And where the body cannott lye
On wings of wynde my soule shall flye:
If not one soul our bodies joyne,
One body shall our soules confine,
    Go wynde and blow thou where thou please,
    Yea breathles leave mee to my ease.

SONG: ON THE BATHS

What Angel stirrs this happy Well,
    Some Muse from thence come shew't me,
One of those naked Graces tell
    That Angels are for beauty:
The Lame themselves that enter here
    Come Angels out againe,
And Bodies turne to Soules all cleere,
    All made for joy, noe payne.

Heate never was so sweetely mett
    With moist as in this shower:
Old men are borne anew by swett
    Of its restoring pow'r:
When crippl'd joynts we suppl'd see,
    And second lives new come,
Who can deny this Font to be
    The Bodies Christendome?

One Bath so fiery is you'l thinke
    The Water is all Spirit,
Whose quick'ning streames are like the drink
    Whereby we Life inheritt:
The second Poole of middle straine
    Can wive Virginity,
Tempting the blood to such a vayne
    One sexe is He and She.

The third where horses plunge may bring
    A Pegasus to reare us,
And call for pens from Bladud's wing
    For legging those that beare us.
Why should Physitians thither fly
    Where Waters med'cines be,

Physitians come to cure thereby,
  And are more cured than we

SONG: A STRANGE GENTLEWOMAN PASSING BY HIS WINDOW

As I out of a casement sent
Mine eyes as wand'ring as my thought,
Upon no certayne object bent,
But only what occasion brought,
A sight surpriz'd my hart at last,
Nor knewe I well what made it burne;
Amazement held me then so fast
I had no leasure to discerne.

Sure 'twas a Mortall, but her name,
Or happy parentage or place,
Or (that which did mee most inflame)
I cannot tell her very Face:
No; 'twere prophane to think I could,
And I should pitch my thoughts too lowe
If ever sett my love I should
On that which Art or Words can shewe.

Was ever man so vext before,
Or ever love so blind as this,
Which vows and wishes to implore,
And yet not knows for what to wish?
Thus children spend theyr wayward cryes,
Not knowing why they doe complayne;
Thus sicke men long for remedyes,
Not knowing what would ease theyr payne.

Some god call backe againe that sight;
Ile suffer double payne to boote,
For griefe and anger in mee fight
So strongly at no marke to shoote!
Not only meanes to winne her grace,
But meanes to seeke are barr'd from mee;

Despayre enforc't by such a case
Is not a sinne but miserie.

Pygmalion hold thine Image fast,
'Tis something to enjoy Love so:
Narcissus thou a shaddowe hast,
At least thereby to cheate thy woe;
But I no likenesse can inferre
My pyning fancy to supply;
Nothing to love instead of her
For feare of some idolatry.

SONG: ON A FRIENDS ABSENCE

Come, come, I faint: thy heavy stay
Doubles each houre of the day:
The winged hast of nimble love
Makes aged Time not seeme to move:
    Did not the light,
    And then the night
    Instruct my sight
I should believe the Sunne forgot his flight.

Show not the drooping marygold
Whose leaves like grieving amber fold:
My longing nothing can explain
But soule and body rent in twain:
    Did I not moane,
    And sigh and groan,
    And talk alone,
I should believe my soul was gone from home.

She's gone, she's gone, away she's fled,
Within my breast to make her bed,
In me there dwels her tenant woe,
And sighs are all the breath I blow:
    Then come to me,
    One touch of thee
    Will make me see
If loving thee I live or dead I be.

Song: Melancholly

Hence, hence, all you vaine delights,
As short as are the nights
Wherein you spend your folly:
Ther's nought in this life sweete,
If men were wise to see'te
But only Melancholly:
    O sweetest Melancholly!

Welcome folded armes and fixed eyes,
A sigh that piercing mortifies,
A looke that's fastned to the ground,
A tongue chayned upp without a sound.
Fountains heads, and pathlesse groves,
Places which pale Passion loves:
Moonlike wakes, when all the Fowles
Are warmly housde, save Batts and Owles:
A midnight knell: a parting groane:
These are the sounds wee feede upon.
Then, stretch your bones in a still gloomy vally,
Ther's nothing daynty, sweete, save Melancholly.

Song: Opposite to Melancholy

Returne my joyes, and hither bring
A tongue not made to speake but sing,
A jolly spleene, an inward feast,
A causelesse laugh without a jest,
A face which gladnesse doth anoynt,
An arm that springs out of his joynt,
A sprightfull gate that leaves no print,
And makes a feather of a flint,
A heart that's lighter than the ayre,
An eye still dancing in his spheare,
Strong mirth which nothing can controule,
A body nimbler than the soule,
Free wandring thoughts not tyde to muse
Which thinke on all things, nothing choose,
Which ere we see them come are gone;
These life itselfe doth feede upon.

A TRANSLATION OF THE NIGHTINGALE OUT OF STRADA

Now the declining sun 'gan downwards bend
From higher heavens, and from his locks did send
A milder flame, when near to Tiber's flow
A lutinist allay'd his careful woe
With sounding charms, and in a greeny seat
Of shady oake took shelter from the heat.
A Nightingale oreheard him, that did use
To sojourn in the neighbour groves, the muse
That fill'd the place, the Syren of the wood;
Poore harmless Syren, stealing neare she stood
Close lurking in the leaves attentively
Recording that unwonted melody:
Shee cons it to herselfe and every strayne
His finger playes her throat return'd again.
The lutinist perceives an answeare sent
From th' imitating bird and was content
To shewe her play; more fully then in haste
He tries his lute, and (giving her a tast
Of the ensuing quarrel) nimbly beats
On all his strings; as nimbly she repeats,
And (wildely ranging ore a thousand keys)
Sends a shrill warning of her after-layes.
With rolling hand the Lutinist then plies
His trembling threads; sometimes in scornful wise
He brushes down the strings and keemes them all
With one even stroke; then takes them severall
And culles them ore again. His sparkling joynts
(With busy descant mincing on the points)
Reach back with busy touch: that done hee stayes,
The bird replies, and art with art repayes,
Sometimes as one unexpert or in doubt
How she might wield her voice, shee draweth out
Her tone at large and doth at first prepare

A solemne strayne not weav'd with sounding ayre,
But with an equall pitch and constant throate
Makes clear the passage of her gliding noate;
Then crosse division diversely shee playes,
And loudly chanting out her quickest layes
Poises the sounds, and with a quivering voice
Falls back again: he (wondering how so choise,
So various harmony should issue out
From such a little throate) doth go about
Some harder lessons, and with wondrous art
Changing the strings, doth upp the treble dart,
And downwards smites the base; with painefull stroke
Hee beats, and as the trumpet doth provoke
Sluggards to fight, even so his wanton skill
With mingled discords joynes the hoarse and shrill:
The Bird this also tunes, and while she cutts
Sharp notes with melting voice, and mingled putts
Measures of middle sound, then suddenly
Shee thunders deepe, and juggs it inwardly,
With gentle murmurs, cleare and dull shee sings,
By course, as when the martial warning rings:
Beleev't the minstrel blusht; with angry mood
Inflam'd, quoth hee, thou chauntresse of the wood,
Either from thee Ile beare the prize away,
Or vanquisht break my lute without delay.
Inimitable accents then hee straynes;
His hand flyes ore the strings: in one hee chaynes
Four different numbers, chasing here and there,
And all the strings belabour'd everywhere:
Both flatt and sharpe hee strikes, and stately grows
To prouder straynes, and backwards as he goes
Doubly divides, and closing upp his layes
Like a full quire a shouting consort playes;
Then pausing stood in expectation
If his corrival now dares answeare on;

But shee when practice long her throate had whett,
Induring not to yield, at once doth sett
Her spiritt all of worke, and all in vayne;
For while shee labours to express againe
With nature's simple touch such diverse keyes,
With slender pipes such lofty noates as these,
Orematcht with high designes, orematcht with woe,
Just at the last encounter of her foe
Shee faintes, shee dies, falls on his instrument
That conquer'd her; a fitting monument.
    So far even little soules are driven on,
    Struck with a vertuous emulation.

ON WESTWELL DOWNES

When Westwell Downes I gan to tread,
Where cleanely wynds the greene did sweepe,
Methought a landskipp there was spread,
Here a bush and there a sheepe:
    The pleated wrinkles of the face
    Of wave-swolne earth did lend such grace,
    As shadowings in Imag'ry
    Which both deceive and please the eye.

The sheepe sometymes did tread the maze
By often wynding in and in,
And sometymes round about they trace
Which milkmayds call a Fairie ring:
    Such semicircles have they runne,
    Such lynes across so trymly spunnne
    That sheppeards learne whenere they please
    A new Geometry with ease.

The slender food upon the downe
Is allwayes even, allwayes bare,
Which neither spring nor winter's frowne
Can ought improve or ought impayre:
    Such is the barren Eunuches chynne,
    Which thus doth evermore begynne
    With tender downe to be orecast
    Which never comes to haire at last.

Here and there twoe hilly crests
Amiddst them hugg a pleasant greene,
And these are like twoe swelling breasts
That close a tender fall betweene.
    Here would I sleepe, or read, or pray
    From early morne till flight of day:

But harke! a sheepe-bell calls mee upp,
Like Oxford colledge bells, to supp.

On a great hollow Tree

Preethee stand still awhile, and view this tree
Renown'd and honour'd for antiquitie
By all the neighbour twiggs; for such are all
The trees adjoyning, bee they nere so tall,
Comparde to this: if here Jacke Maypole stood
All men would sweare 'twere but a fishing rodde.
Mark but the gyant trunk, which when you see
You see how many woods and groves there bee
Compris'd within one elme. The hardy stocke
Is knotted like a clubb, and who dares mocke
His strength by shaking it? Each brawny limbe
Could pose the centaure Monychus, or him
That wav'de a hundred hands ere hee could wield
That sturdy waight, whose large extent might shield
A poore man's tenement. Greate Ceres' oake
Which Erisichthon feld, could not provoke
Halfe so much hunger for his punishment
As hewing this would doe by consequent.
    Nothing but age could tame it: Age came on,
And loe a lingering consumption
Devour'd the entralls, where an hollow cave
Without the workman's helpe began to have
The figure of a Tent: a pretty cell
Where grand Silenus might not scorne to dwell,
And owles might feare to harbour, though they brought
Minerva's warrant for to bear them out
In this their bold attempt. Looke down into
The twisted curles, the wreathing to and fro
Contrived by nature: where you may descry
How hall and parlour, how the chambers lie.
And wer't not strange to see men stand alone
On leggs of skinne without or flesh or bone?
Or that the selfe same creature should survive

After the heart is dead? This tree can thrive
Thus maym'd and thus impayr'd: no other proppe,
But only barke remayns to keep it uppe.
Yet thus supported it doth firmly stand,
Scorning the saw-pitt, though so neere at hand.
No yawning grave this grandsire Elme can fright,
Whilst yongling trees are martyr'd in his sight.
O learne the thrift of Nature, that maintaines
With needy myre stolne upp in hidden veynes
So great a bulke of wood. Three columnes rest
Upon the rotten trunke, whereof the least
Were mast for Argos. Th' open backe below
And three long leggs alone doe make it shew
Like a huge trivett, or a monstrous chayre
With the heeles turn'd upward. How proper, ô how fayre
A seate were this for old Diogenes
To grumble in and barke out oracles,
And answere to the Raven's augury
That builds above. Why grew not this strange tree
Neere Delphos? had this wooden majesty
Stood in Dodona forest, then would Jove
Foregoe his oake, and only this approve.
Had those old Germans that did once admire
Deformed Groves; and worshipping with fire
Burnt men unto theyr gods: had they but seene
These horrid stumps, they canonizde had beene,
And highly too. This tree would calme more gods
Than they had men to sacrifice by odds.
        You Hamadryades, that wood-borne bee,
Tell mee the causes, how this portly tree
Grew to this haughty stature? Was it then
Because the mummys of so many men
Fattned the ground? or cause the neighbor spring
Conduits of water to the roote did bring?
Was it with Whitsun sweat, or ample snuffes

Of my Lord's beere that such a bignesse stuffs
And breaks the barke? O this it is, no doubt:
This tree, I warrant you, can number out
Your Westwell annals, & distinctly tell
The progresse of this hundred years, as well
By Lords and Ladies, as ere Rome could doe
By Consulships. These boughes can witnesse too
How goodman Berry trippt it in his youth,
And how his daughter Joane, of late forsooth
Became her place. It might as well have grown,
If Pan had pleas'd, on top of Westwell downe,
Instead of that proud Ash; and easily
Have given ayme to travellers passing by
With wider armes. But see, it more desirde
Here to bee lov'd at home than there admirde:
And porter-like it here defends the gate,
As if it once had been greate Askapate.
Had warlike Arthur's dayes enjoy'd this Elme
Sir Tristram's blade and good Sir Lancelot's helme
Had then bedeckt his locks, with fertile store
Of votive reliques which those champions wore:
Untill perhaps (as 'tis with great men found)
Those burdenous honours crusht it to the ground:
But in these merry times 'twere farre more trimme
If pipes and citterns hung on every limbe;
And since the fiddlers it hath heard so long,
I'me sure by this time it deserves my song.

On Fayrford Windowes

I know no paynt of poetry
Can mend such colourd Imag'ry
In sullen inke: yet Fayrford, I
May relish thy fayre memory.
    Such is the Ecchoes faynter sound,
Such is the light when sunne is drownd;
So did the fancy looke upon
The worke before it was begunne:
Yet when those shewes are out of sight
My weaker colours may delight.
    Those Images so faythfully
Report true feature to the eye
As you may thinke each picture was
Some visage in a looking-glasse;
Not a glasse-window face, unlesse
Such as Cheapside hath: where a presse
Of paynted gallants looking out
Bedecke the Casement round about:
But these have holy physnomy:
Each pane instructs the Laity
With silent eloquence: for here
Devotion leads the eye, not eare,
To note the catechising paynt,
Whose easy phrase doth so acquaint
Our sense with Gospell that the Creede
In such a hand the weake may reade:
Such types even yet of vertue be,
And Christ, as in a glasse wee see.
    Behold two turtles in one cage,
With such a lovely equipage,
As they who knew them long may doubt
Some yong ones have bin stollen out.
    When with a fishing rodde the clarke

Saint Peters draught of fish doth marke,
Such is the scale, the eye, the finne,
Youd thinke they strive and leape within;
But if the nett, which holds them breake,
Hee with his angle some would take.

    But would you walke a turne in Pauls?
Looke uppe; one little pane inroules
A fayrer temple: fling a stone
The Church is out o' the windowes throwne.

    Consider, but not aske your eyes,
And ghosts at midday seeme to rise:
The Saynts there, striving to descend,
Are past the glasse, and downward bend.

    Looke there! The Divell! all would cry
Did they not see that Christ was by:
See where he suffers for thee: see
His body taken from the Tree:
Had ever death such life before?
The limber corps, besullyd ore
With meager palenesse, doth display
A middle state twixt Flesh and Clay:
His armes and leggs, his head and crowne,
Like a true Lambskinne dangling downe,
Who can forbeare, the Grave being nigh,
To bring fresh oyntment in his eye?

    The wondrous art hath equall fate,
Unfenced and yet unviolate:
The Puritans were sure deceivd,
And thought those shadowes movde and heavde,
So held from stoning Christ: the winde
And boystrous tempests were so kinde
As on his Image not to prey,
Whom both the winds and seas obey.

    At Momus wish bee not amazd;
For if each Christian heart were glazde

With such a window, then each breast
Might bee his owne Evangelist.

On a Gentlewoman's blistred lipp

Hide not that sprouting lipp, nor kill
The juicy bloome with bashfull skill:
Know it is an amorous dewe
That swells to court thy corall hewe,
And what a blemish you esteeme
To other eyes a pearle may seeme
Whose watery growth is not above
The thrifty seize that pearles doe love,
And doth so well become that part
That chance may seeme a secret art.
Doth any judge that face lesse fayre
Whose tender silke a mole doth beare?
Or will a diamond shine less cleare
If in the midst a soil appeare?
Or else that eye a finer nett
Whose glass is ring'd about with jett?
Or is an apple thought more sweete
When hony specks and redde doe meet?
         Then is the lipp made fayrer by
         Such sweetness of deformitie
The nectar which men strive to sipp
Springs like a well upon your lipp,
Nor doth it shew immodesty,
But overflowing chastity.
O who will blame the fruitfull trees
When too much sapp and gumme hee sees?
Here nature from her store doth send
Only what other parts can lend;
The budde of love which here doth growe
Were too too sweete if pluckt belowe;
When lovely buddes ascend so high
The roote belowe cannot be drye.

To a Gentlewoman for a Friend

No marvell if the Sunne's bright eye
Shower downe hott flames; that qualitie
Still waytes on light; but when wee see
Those sparkling balles of ebony
Distil such heat, the gazer straight
Stands so amazed at the sight
As when the lightning makes a breach
Through pitchie clouds: can lightning reach
The marrowe hurting not the skynne?
Your eyes to me the same have byn;
Can jett invite the loving strawe
With secrett fire? so those can draw,
And can, where ere they glance a dart,
Make stubble of the strongest hart.
Oft when I looke I may descry
A little face peep through your eye;
Sure 'tis the boy, who wisely chose
His throne among such rayes as those,
Which, if his quiver chance to fail,
May serve for darts to kill withal:
If to such powerful shafts I yeild,
If with so many wounds I bleed,
Think me noe coward, though I lye
Thus prostrate with your charming eye:
Did I say but your eye? I sweare
Death's in your beauty everywhere.
Your waxen hands when I recall,
Your lily breasts, their melting vale,
Your damaske cheeks, your lilly skynne,
Your corral lipp and dainty chynne,
Your shining locks and amber breath,
All pleasing instruments of death,
Your eye may spare itselfe: mine owne

When all your parts are duly knowne
From any part may fetch a dart
To wound itselfe. Kill not my hart,
By saying that I will dispise
The parentage from which you rise:
I know it well, and likewise knowe
That I my myselfe my breath doe owe
To Woolsey's roofe, and can it bee
I should disdayne your pedigree?
Or is your Sire a butcher found?
The fitter you to make a wound;
Wound mee againe and more and more,
So you againe will mee restore,
But if resemblance tell the father
I think hee was an Angell rather.

For a Gentleman, who, kissinge his Friend at his departure left a signe of blood on her

What mystery was this; that I should finde
My blood in kissing you to stay behinde?
'Twas not for want of color that requirde
My blood for paynt: No dye could be desirde
On that fayre silke, where scarlett were a spott
And where the juice of lillies but a blotte.
'Twas not the signe of murther that did taynt
The harmlesse beauty of so pure a saynt:
Yes, of a loving murther, which rough steele
Could never worke; such as we joy to feele:
Wherby the ravisht soule though dying lives,
Since life and death the selfsame object gives.
If at the presence of a murtherer
The wound will bleede and tell the cause is ther,
A touch will doe much more, and thus my heart,
When secretly it felt the killing darte,
Shew'd it in blood: which yet doth more complayne
Because it cannot be so touched againe.
This wounded heart, to shew its love most true,
Sent forth a droppe and writ its minde on you.
Never was paper halfe so white as this,
Nor waxe so yeelding to the printed kisse,
Nor seal'd so strong. Noe letter ere was writt
That could the author's minde so truly hitt.
For though myselfe to foreigne countries flie,
My blood desires to keepe you company.
Here could I spill it all: thus I can free
Mine enemy from blood, though slayne I be:
But slayne I cannot bee, nor meete with ill,
Since but by you I have no blood to spill.

On a Dissembler

Could any shewe where Plynyes people dwell
Whose head stands in their breast; who cannot tell
A smoothing lye because their open hart
And lippes are join'd so neare, I would depart
As quick as thought, and there forgett the wrongs
Which I have suffer'd by deceitfull tongues.
I should depart where soules departed bee,
Who being freed from cloudy flesh, can see
Each other so immediately, so cleare
That none needs tongue to speak, nor ears to hear.
Were tongues intended to express the soule,
And can wee better doe't with none at all?
Were words first made our meaning to reveale,
And are they usde our meaning to conceale?
The ayre by which wee see, will that turne fogg?
Our breath turne mist? Will that become a clogg
That should unload the mind? Fall we upon
Another Babell's sub-confusion?
And in the self-same language must wee finde
A diverse faction of the words and minde?
Dull as I am, that hugg'd such emptie ayre,
And never mark't the deede (a phrase more faire,
More trusty and univocall): joyne well
Three or foure actions, we may quickly spell
A hollow hart: if those no light can lend
Read the whole sentence, and observe the end:
I will not wayte so long: the guilded man
On whom I ground my speech, no longer can
Delude my sense; nor can the gracefull arte
Of kind dissembling button upp his hart.
His well-spoke wrongs are such as hurtfull words
Writt in a comely hand; or bloody swords
Sheath'd upp in velvett; if hee draw on mee
My armour proofe is incredulity.

ON GRAY EYES

Looke how the russet morne exceeds the night,
How sleekest Jett yields to the di'monds light,
So farr the glory of the gray-bright eye
Out-vyes the black in lovely majesty.
A morning mantl'd with a fleece of grey
Laughs from her brow and shewes a spotlesse day:
This di'mond-like doth not his lustre owe
To borrowed helpe, as black thinges cast a show,
It needs noe day besides itselfe, and can
Make a Cimmeria seeme meridian:
Light sees, tis seen, tis that whereby wee see
When darknesse in the opticke facultie
Is but a single element: then tell
Is not that eye the best wherein doth dwell
More plenteous light? that organ is divine,
And more than eye that is all chrystalline,
All rich of sight: oh that perspicuous glasse
That lets in light, and lets a light forth passe
Tis Lustre's thoroughfare where rayes doe thronge,
A burning glasse that fires the lookers-on.
Black eies set off coarse beauties which they grace
But as a beard smutch'd on a swarthy face.
Why should the seat of life be dull'd with shade,
Or that be darke for which the day was made?
The learned Pallas, who had witt to choose,
And power to take, did other eyes refuse,
And wore the gray: each country painter blotts
His goddesse eyeballs with two smutty spotts.
Corruption layes on blacke; give me the eye
Whose lustre dazles paynt and poetrie,
That's day unto itselfe; which like the sun
Seemes all one flame. They that his beames will shun
Here die like flyes: when eyes of every kind

Faint at the sun, at these the sun growes blind,
And skipps behind a cloud, that all may say
The Eye of all the world loves to be gray.

On a Gentlewoman's Watch that Wanted a Key

Thou pretty heav'n whose great and lesser spheares
With constant wheelings measure hours and yeares
Soe faithfully that thou couldst solve the doubt
Of erring Time if Nature should be out,
Where's thy intelligence? thy Soule? the Key
That gives thee Life and Motion? must thou stay
Thus cramp'd with rusty sloth? and shall each wheel
Disorganis'd confess it is but steele?
Art's Living Creature, is thy thread all spent?
Thy Pulse quite dead? hath Time a period sent
To his owne Sister? slaine his Eeven Match?
That when we look 'tis doomesday by the Watch.
Prithee sweete Watch be marri'd, joyne thy side
Unto an active key, and then abide
A frequent screwing, till successively
More and more Time beget Eternity.
Knowe as a woman never lock'd and key'd
Once in twice twelve growes faint and is downe-weighed
From Nature's full intent, and cannot live
Beyond her natural span, unlesse Man give
His vanish'd bone a quick'ning, unless Man
Doe adde an Ell unto her now shrunk span,
Unless he lengthen out posteritie
Her secret orbes will faint and She all die;
Soe will thy wheeles decay, and finde their date
Unless a Key their houres doe propagate:
Then gett a key and live; my life Ile gage
Each minute then shall grow into an age;
Then lett thy Mistresse looking smile on Thee,
And say 'tis time my Watch and I agree.

A Watch sent home to Mrs. Eliz: King, wrappt in these Verses

Goe and count her better houres;
They more happie are than ours.
The day that gives her any blisse
Make it as long againe as tis:
The houre shee smiles in lett it bee
By thy art increas'd to three:
But if shee frowne on thee or mee
Know night is made by her not thee:
Bee swift in such an houre, and soon
Make it night though it bee noone:
Obey her tymes, who is the free
Fayre sun that governes thee and me.

On a watch made by a Blacksmith

A Vulcan and a Venus seldom part.
A blacksmith never us'd to filinge art
Beyond a lock and key, for Venus' sake
Hath cut a watch soe small that sence will ache
In searching every wire, and subtile sphere
Which his industrious skill hath order'd theire:
It scarce outswells a nut, and is soe light
A Ladies eare might well indure the weight.
Twas for a Mistresse: pitty not his owne,
And yet not pitty when her worth is knowne,
Or els his love that ownes her: Either's name
Is carv'd within the plates: the witty frame
Hath made their letters kiss for them, while they
Have like the watch one pulse, one sympathy.

On a Gentlewoman
that sung and play'd upon a Lute

Be silent you still musique of the Sphears,
And every sense make haste to be all ears,
And give devout attention to her aires,
To which the Gods doe listen as to prayers
Of pious votaries; the which to heare
Tumult would be attentive, and would swear
To keep less noise at Nile, if there she sing,
Or with a happy touch grace but the string.
Among so many auditors, such throngs
Of Gods and men that presse to hear her songs,
O let me have an unespied room,
And die with such an anthem ore my tomb

Upon the blush of a faire Ladie

Stay lusty blood! where canst thou seeke
So blest a seat as in her cheeke?
How dar'st thou from her face retire
Whose beauty doth command desire?
But if thou wilt not stay, then flowe
Downe to her panting pappes belowe:
There take thou glory to distayne
With azure blewe each swelling veyne,
From thence run boyling through each part
Till thou hast warm'd her frozen hart,
Which, if from love thou find'st entire,
O martyr it with gentle fire.

ON A GENTLEWOMAN WALKING IN THE SNOWE

I saw fair Cloris walke alone
Where feather'd rayne came softly downe,
And Jove descended from his tower
To court her in a silver shower;
The wanton snowe flewe to her breast
Like little birds into their nest,
And overcome with whiteness there
For greife it thaw'd into a teare,
Thence falling on her garment's hemme
For greife it freez'd into a gemme.

ON CHLORIS STANDING BY THE FIRE

Fair Chloris, standing by the Fire,
An amorous coale with hot desire
Leapt on her breast, but could not melt
The chaste snow there—which when it felt
For shame it blusht; and then it died
There where resistance did abide,
And lest she should take it unkind
Repentant ashes left behind.

To a Valentine

Faire Valentine, since once your welcome hand
Did cull mee out wrapt in a paper band,
Vouchsafe the same hand still, to shew thereby
That Fortune did your will no injury:
What though a knife I give, your beauty's charme
Will keepe the edge from doing any harme:
Wool deads the sternest blade; and will not such
A weake edge turn, meeting a softer touch?

A Superscription on Sir Philip Sidney's *Arcadia*, Sent for a Token

Whatever in Philoclea the fair
Or the discreet Pamela figur'd are,
Change but the name the virtues are your owne,
And for a fiction there a truth is knowne:
If any service here perform'd you see,
If duty and affection paynted bee
Within these leaves: may you be pleas'd to know
They only shadow what I truly owe
To your desart: thus I a glasse have sent
Which both myself and you doth represent.

On the Picture of two Dolphins in a Fountayne

These dolphins twisting each on either side
For joy leaped upp, and gazing there abide;
And whereas other waters fish doe bring,
Here from the fishes doe the waters spring,
Who think it is more glorious to give
Than to receive the juice whereby they live:
And by this milk-white bason learne you may
That pure hands you should bring or beare away,
For which the bason wants no furniture,
Each dolphin wayting makes his mouth an ewer,
Your welcome then you well may understande
When fish themselves give water to your hand.

Sonnett

My love and I for kisses play'd,
She would keepe stake, I was content,
But when I wonne shee would be paid;
This made mee aske her what she meant.
Pray, since I see (quoth shee) your wrangling vayne,
Take your own kisses, give me myne againe.

To his Mistresse

In your sterne beauty I can see
Whatere in Ætna wonders bee;
If coales out of the topp doe flye
Hott flames doe gush out of your eye;
If frost lye on the ground belowe
Your breast is white and cold as snowe:
The sparkes that sett my hart on fire
Refuse to melt your owne desire:
The frost that byndes your chilly breast
With double fire hath mee oppresst:
Both heate and cold a league have made,
And leaving you they mee invade:
The hearth its proper flame withstands
When ice itselfe heates others hands.

A Lover to his Mistress

Ile tell you how the Rose did first grow redde,
And whence the Lilly whitenesse borrowed:
You blusht, and then the Rose with redde was dight:
The Lillies kissde your hands, and so came white:
Before that time each Rose had but a stayne,
The Lilly nought but palenesse did contayne:
You have the native colour, these the dye;
They flourish only in your livery.

A Riddle: on a Kiss

What thing is that, nor felt nor seene
Till it bee given? a present for a Queene:
A fine conceite to give and take the like:
The giver yet is farther for to seeke;
The taker doth possesse nothing the more,
The giver hee hath nothing lesse in store:
And given once that nature hath it still,
You cannot keepe or leave it if you will:
The workmanshippe is counted very small,
The labour is esteemed naught at all:
But to conclude, this gift is such indeede,
That, if some see't 'twill make theyr hearts to bleede.

On a Gentlewoman that had had the small poxe

A Beauty smoother than the Ivory playne
Late by the Poxe injuriously was slayne:
Twas not the Poxe: Love shott a thousand darts,
And made those pitts for graves to bury hearts:
But since that Beauty hath regaynde her light,
Those hearts are double slayne, it shines so bright.

On Jealousy

There is a thing that nothing is,
A foolish wanton, sober wise;
It hath noe wings, noe eyes, noe eares,
And yet it flies, it sees, it heares;
It lives by losse, it feeds on smart,
It joyes in woe, it liveth not;
Yet evermore this hungry elfe
Doth feed on nothing but itselfe.

Of Death & Resurrection

Like to the rowling of an eye,
Or like a starre shot from the skye,
Or like a hand upon a clock,
Or like a wave upon a rock,
Or like a winde, or like a flame,
Or like false newes which people frame,
Even such is man, of equall stay,
Whose very growth leades to decay.
    The eye is turn'd, the starre down bendeth
    The hand doth steale, the wave descendeth,
    The wind is spent, the flame unfir'd,
    The newes disprov'd, man's life expir'd.

Like to an eye which sleepe doth chayne,
Or like a starre whose falle we fayne,
Or like the shade on Ahaz watch,
Or like a wave which gulfes doe snatch
Or like a winde or flame that's past,
Or smother'd newes confirm'd at last;
Even so man's life, pawn'd in the grave,
Wayts for a riseing it must have.
    The eye still sees, the star still blazeth,
    The shade goes back, the wave escapeth,
    The winde is turn'd, the flame reviv'd,
    The newes renew'd, and man new liv'd.

ON THE BIBLE

Behold this little volume here inrolde:
'Tis the Almighty's present to the world:
Hearken earth's earth; each sencelesse thing can heare
His Maker's thunder, though it want an eare:
God's word is senior to his works, nay rather
If rightly weigh'd the world may call it father;
God spake, 'twas done; this great foundation
Is the Creator's Exhalation
Breath'd out in speaking. The best work of man
Is better than his word; but if wee scanne
God's word aright, his works far short doe fall;
The word is God, the works are creatures all.
The sundry peeces of this generall frame
Are dimmer letters, all which spell the same
Eternal word; But these cannot expresse
His greatnesse with such easy readinesse,
And therefore yeild. The Heavens shall pass away,
The sun and moone and stars shall all obey
To light one general bonfire; but his word,
His builder-upp, his all-destroying sworde,
That still survives; no jott of that can dye,
Each tittle measures immortalitie.
    The word's owne mother, on whose breast did hang
The world's upholder drawne into a span,
Shee, shee was not so blest because she bare him
As cause herselfe was new-born, and did hear him.
Before she had brought forth she heard her Son
First speaking in the Annunciation:
And then, even then, before she brought forth child,
By name of Blessed shee herselfe instilde.
    Once more this mighty word his people greets,
Thus lapt and thus swath'd upp in paper sheets:
Read here God's Image with a zealous eye,
The legible and written Deity.

On a Register for the Bible

I am the faythfull deputy
Unto your fading memory.
Your Index long in search doth hold;
Your folded wrinkles make books olde:
But I the Scripture open plaine,
And what you heard soone teach againe:
By me the Welchman well may bring
Himselfe to Heaven in a string.

Anthem for Good Fryday

See sinfull soul thy Saviours suffering see,
His Blessed hands and feet fix't fast to tree:
Observe what Rivulets of blood stream forth
His painful pierced side, each drop more worth
Than tongue of men and Angels can express:
Hast to him, cursed Caitiffe, and confess
All thy misdeeds, and sighing say, 'Twas I
That caused thee thus, my Lord, my Christ, to dye.

O let thy Death secure my soul from fears,
And I will wash thy wounds with brinish tears:
Grant me, sweet Jesu, from thy pretious store
One cleansing drop, with grace to sin no more.

An Antheme

O sing a new song to the Lord,
Praise in the hight and deeper strayne;
Come beare your parts with one accord,
Which you in Heaven may sing againe.

Yee elders all, and all the crowd
That in white robes apparell'd stands
Like Saints on earth, sing out aloud,
Think now the palmes are in your hands.

Yee living pipes, whose stormy layes
Have borrowed breath to praise our king,
A well-tun'd thunder loudly raise:
All that have breath his honour sing.

Justification

See how the Rainbow in the skie
Seems gaudy through the Suns bright eye;
Harke how an Eccho answere makes,
Feele how a board is smooth'd with waxe,
Smell how a glove putts on perfume,
Tast how their sweetnesse pills assume:
So by imputed Justice, Clay
Seemes faire, well spoke, smooth, sweet, each way.
    The eye doth gaze on robes appearing,
    The prompted Eccho takes our hearing,
    The board our touch, the sent our smell,
    The pill our tast: Man, God as well.

On the Life of Man

What is our life? a play of passion;
Our mirth the musick of division:
Our mother's wombes the tyring houses be
Where wee are drest for tyme's short comedy:
The earth's the stage, heaven the spectator is,
Who marketh still whoere doth act amisse:
Our graves that hide us from the burning sunne
Are but drawne curtaynes when the play is done.

On the Death of Mrs. Mary Neudham

As sinn makes gross the soule and thickens it
To fleshy dulness, so the spotless white
Of virgin pureness made thy flesh as cleere
As others soules: thou couldst not tarry heere
All soule in both parts: and what could it bee
The Resurrection could bestow on thee,
Allready glorious? thine Innocence
(Thy better shroude) sent thee as pure from hence
As saints shall rise: but hee whose bounty may
Enlighten the greate sunn with double day,
And make it more outshine itselfe than now
It can the moone, shall crowne thy varnish'd brow
With light above that sunn: when thou shalt bee
No lower in thy place than Majesty:
Crown'd with a Virgin's wreath, outshining there
The Saints as much as thou did'st mortalls heere.
Bee this thy hope; and whilst thy ashes ly
Asleepe in death, dreame of Eternity.

On the Death of Mistress Mary Prideaux

Weep not because this childe hath dyed so young,
But weep because yourselves have livde so long:
Age is not fild by growth of time, for then
What old man lives to see th' estate of men?
Who sees the age of grande Methusalem?
Ten years make us as old as hundreds him.
Ripenesse is from ourselves: and then wee dye
When nature hath obteynde maturity.
Summer and winter fruits there bee, and all
Not at one time, but being ripe, must fall.
Death did not erre: your mourners are beguilde;
She dyed more like a mother than a childe.
Weigh the composure of her pretty partes:
Her gravity in childhood; all her artes
Of womanly behaviour; weigh her tongue
So wisely measurde, not too short nor long;
And to her youth adde some few riches more,
She tooke upp now what due was at threescore.
She livde seven years, our age's first degree;
Journeys at first time ended happy bee;
Yet take her stature with the age of man,
They well are fitted: both are but a span.

On the same M. M. P.

Sleepe pretty one: oh sleepe while I
Sing thee thy latest Lullaby:
And may my song be but as shee,
Nere was sweeter Harmonie:
Thou werte all musicke: all thy limbes
Were but so many well sett hymnes
To prayse thy Maker. In thy browe
I read thy soule, and and know not how
To tell which whiter was or smoother,
Or more spotlesse, one or th' other.
Noe jarre, no harshnesse in thee: all
Thy passions were at peace: noe gall,
No rough behaviour; but even such
In disposition as in touch.
Yet Heaven poore Soule, was harsh to thee:
Death usde thee not halfe orderly:
If thou must needs goe, must thy way
Needs be by torture? must thy Day
Ende in the Morning? and thy Night
Come with such horrour and affright?
Death might have ceizd thee gentlyer, and
Embrac'te thee with a softer hand.
Thou werte not sure so loath to goe
That thou needst be dragged so,
For thou wert all obedience, and hadst witt
To doe Heaven's will and not dispute with it.
Yet twere a heard heart, a dead eye
That sighlesse, tearlesse, could stand by,
While thy poore Mother felt each groane
As much as ere shee did her owne
When shee groan'd for thee: and thy cries
Marrde not our eares more than her Eyes.
Yet if thou tookst some truce with payne,

Then was shee melted more againe
To heare thy sweete words, whilst thy breath
Faintly did strive to sweeten Death,
Calldst for the Musicke of thy knell,
And crydst, 'twas It must make thee well:
Thus whilst your prayers were at strife,
Thine for thy death, Hers for thy life,
Thine did prevayle, and on theyr wings
Mounted thy soul; where now it sings,
And never shall complayne no more,
But for not being there before.

CONSOLATORIUM, AD PARENTES

Lett her parents then confesse
That they beleeve her happinesse,
Which now they question. Thinke as you
Lent her the world, Heaven lent her you:
And is it just then to complayne
When each hath but his owne againe?
Then thinke what both your glories are
In her preferment: for tis farre
Nobler to gett a Saint, and beare
A child to Heaven than an Heyre
To a large Empire. Thinke beside
Shee dyed not young, but livde a Bride.
Your best wishes for her good
Were but to see her well bestowde:
Was shee not so? Shee marryed to
The heyre of all things: who did owe
Her infant Soule, and bought it too.
Nor was shee barren: markt you not
Those pretty little Graces, that
Play'd round about her sicke bedde; three

Th' eldst Faith, Hope, & Charity.
Twere pretty bigge ones, and the same
That cryde so on theyr Fathers name.
The yongst is gone with Her: the two
Eldest stay to comfort you,
And little though they bee, they can
Master the biggest foes of man.
Lastly thinke that Hir abode
With you was some fewe years boarde;
After hir marriage: now shee's gone
Home, royally attended on:
And if you had Elisha's sight
To see the number of her bright
Attendants thither; or Paul's rapt sprite
To see her Welcome there; why then,
Wish if you could Her here agen.
Ime sure you could not: but all passion
Would loose itselfe in admiration,
And strong longings to be there
Where, cause shee is, you mourn for her.

HER EPITAPH

Happy Grave, thou dost enshrine
That which makes thee a rich mine:
Remember yet, 'tis but a loane;
And wee must have it back, Her owne,
The very same; Marke mee, the same:
Thou canst not cheat us with a lame
Deformed Carcase; Shee was fayre,
Fresh as Morning, sweete as Ayre:
Purer than other flesh as farre
As other Soules than Bodies are:
And that thou mayst the better see

To finde her out: two stars there bee
Eclipsed now; uncloude but those
And they will poynt thee to the Rose
That dyde each cheeke, now pale and wan,
But will bee when she wakes againe
Fresher than ever: And howere
Her long sleepe may alter Her
Her Soule will know her Body streight,
Twas made so fitt for't. Noe deceite
Can suite another to it: none
Clothe it so neatly as its owne.

On the Death of Sir Tho: Peltham

Merely for man's death to mourne
Were to repine that man was borne.
When weake old age doth fall asleepe
Twere foule ingratitude to weepe:
Those threads alone should pull out tears
Whose sodayne cracke breaks off some years.
Heere tis not so: full distance heere
Sunders the cradle from the beere.
A fellow-traveller he hath beene
So long with Time: so worne to skinne,
That were hee not just now bereft,
His Body first his soule had left,
Threescore and tenne is Nature's date,
Our journey when wee come in late.
Beyond that time the overplus
Was granted not to him, but us.
For his own sake the Sun nere stood,
But only for the peoples good.
Even so his breath held out by aire
Which poor men uttered in theyr prayer:
And as his goods were lent to give,
So were his dayes that they might live,
Soe ten years more to him were told
Enough to make another olde.
O that Death would still doe soe;
Or else on good men would bestow
That wast of years which unthrifts fling
Away by theyr distempering,
That some might thrive by this decay
As well as that of land and clay.
'Twas now well done: no cause to moane
On such a seasonable stone.
Where death is but an Host, we sinne

Not bidding welcome to his Inne.
    Sleepe, sleepe, thy rest, good man, embrace;
    Sleepe, sleepe, th'ast trod a weary race.

ON THE DEATH OF A TWIN

Where are yee now, Astrologers, that looke
For petty accidents in Heavens booke?
Two Twins, to whom one Influence gave breath,
Differ in more than Fortune, Life and Death.
While both were warme (for that was all they were
Unlesse some feeble cry sayd Life was there
By wavering change of health they seem'd to trie
Which of the two should live, for one must die.
As if one Soule, allotted to susteine
The lumpe, which afterwards was cutt in twain,
Now servde them both: whose limited restraynt
From double vertue made them both to faynt:
But when that common Soule away should flie,
Death killing one, expected both should die:
Shee hitt, and was deceivde: that other parte
Went to supply the weake survivers heart:
So Death, where shee was cruell, seemde most milde:
She aymed at two, and killed but halfe a childe.

On the yong Baronett Portman
Dying of an Impostume in's Head

Is Death so cunning now that all her blowe
Aymes at the heade? Doth now her wary Bowe
Make surer worke than heertofore? The steele
Slew warlike heroes onely in the heele.
New found out slights, when men themselves begin
To be theyr proper Fates by new found sinne.
Tis cowardize to make a wound so sure;
No Art in killing where no Art can cure.
Was it for hate of learning that she smote
This upper shoppe where all the Muses wrought?
Learning shall crosse her drift, and duly trie
All wayes and meanes of immortalitie.
Because her heade was crusht, doth shee desire
Our equall shame? In vayne she doth aspire.
No: noe: we know where ere shee make a breach
Her poysoned Sting onely the Heele can reach.
Looke on the Soule of man, the very Heart;
The Head itselfe is but a lower parte:
Yet hath shee straynde her utmost tyranny,
And done her worst in that she came so high.
Had she reservde this stroke for haughty men,
For politique Contrivers; justly then
The Punishment were matcht with the offence:
But when Humility and Innocence
So indiscreetly in the Heade are hitt,
Death hath done Murther, and shall die for itt:
Thinke it no Favour showne because the Braine
Is voyde of sence, and therefore free from payne.
Thinke it noe kindness when so stealingly
He rather seemde to jest away than die,
And like that Innocent, the Widdow's childe
Cryde out, My head, my head: and so it dyde.

Thinke it was rather double cruelty,
Slaughter intended on his Name, that Hee
Whose thoughts were nothing taynted, nothing vayne,
Might seeme to hide Corruption in his brayne.
How easy might this Blott be wipte away
If any Pen his worth could open lay?
For which those Harlot-prayses, which we reare
In common dust, as much too slender are
As great for others. Boasting Elegies
Must here bee dumbe. Desert that overweighs
All our Reward stoppes all our Prayse: lest wee
Might seeme to give alike to Them and Thee:
Wherefore an humble Verse, and such a strayne
As mine will hide the truth while others fayne.

On the Death of Dr. Lancton
President of Maudlin College

When men for injuryes unsatisfy'd,
For hopes cut off, for debts not fully payd,
For legacies in vain expected, mourne
Over theyr owne respects within the urne,
Races of tears all striveing first to fall
As frequent are as eye and funerall;
Then high swolne sighes drawne in and sent out strong
Seeme to call back the soule or goe along.
Goodness is seldome such a theam of woe
Unless to her owne tribe some one or two;
But here's a man, (alas a shell of man!)
Whose innocence, more white than silver swan,
Now finds a streame of tears; such perfect greif
That in the traine of mourners hee is cheife
Who lives the greatest gainer; and would faine
Bee now prefer'd unto his losse againe.
The webb of nerves with subtill branches spred
Over the little world, are in theyr head
Scarce so united as in him were knitt
All his dependants: Hee that strives to sitt
So lov'd of all must bee a man as square
As vertues self; which those that fly and feare
Can never hate. How seldome have we seene
Such store of flesh joyn'd with so little sin?
His body was not greater than his soule,
Whose limbs were vertues able to controule
All grudg of sloth: and as the body's weight
Hal'd to the centre; so the soule as light
Heav'd upward to her goale. This civill jarre
Could not hold out, but made them part as farre
As earth and heaven: from whence the one shall come
To make her mate more fresh, less cumbersome.

After so sound a sleepe, so sweet a rest,
And both shall then appeare so trimly drest
As freinds that go to meet: the body shall
Then seeme a soule, the soule Angelicall:
A beautious smile shall passe from that to this,
The joyning soule shall then the body kisse
With its owne lipps: so great shall be the store
Of joy and love that now thei'l part no more;
Such hope hath dust! besides which happines
Death hath not made his earthly share the lesse,
Or quite bereft him of his honors here,
But added more; for liveing hee did steere
The fellowes only; but since hee is dead
Hee's made a president unto theyr head.

On the Death of Sir Thomas Lea

You that affright with lamentable notes
The servants from their beef, whose hungry throats
Vex the grume porter's surly conscience:
That blesse the mint for coyning lesse than pence:
You whose unknown and meanly payd desarts
Begge silently within, and knocke at hearts:
You whose commanding worth makes men beleeve
That you a kindnesse give when you receave:
All sorts of them that want, your tears now lend:
A House-keeper, a Patron, and a Friend
Is lodged in clay. The man whose table fedde
So many while he lived, since hee is dead,
Himselfe is turn'd to food: whose chimney burn'd
So freely then, is now to ashes turn'd.
The man which life unto the Muses gave
Seeks life of them, a lasting Epitaph:
And hee from whose esteeme all vertues found
A just reward, now prostrate in the ground,
(Like some huge ancient oake, that ere it fell,
Could not be measur'd by the rule so well)
Desires a faythfull comment on his dayes,
Such as shall neither lye to wrong or prayse:
But oh! what Muse is halfe so pure, so strong,
What marble sheets can keepe his name so long
As onely hee hath lived? then who can tell
A perfect story of his living well?
The noble fire that spur'd and whetted on
His bravely vertuous resolution
Could not so soone be quenched as weaker soules
Whose feebler sparke an ach or thought controuls.
His life burnt to the snuffe; a snuffe that needs
No socket to conceale the stench, but feeds
Our sence like costly fumes: his manly breath

Felt no disease but age; and call'd for Death
Before it durst intrude, or thought to try
That strength of limbs, that soules integrity.
Looke on his silver hayres, his graceful browe,
And Gravity itselfe might Lea avowe
Her father: Time, his schoolmate. Fifty years
Once wedlocke he embrac't: a date that bears
Fayre scope, if Soule and Body chance to bee
So long a couple as his wife and he.
    But number you his deeds, they so outpasse
The largest size of any mortal glasse,
That though hee liv'd a thousand, some would crye
Alas! he dyde in his minority.
His dayes and deeds would nere be counted even
Without Eternity, which now is given.
Such descants poore men make; who miss him more
Than sixe great men, that keeping house before
After a spurt unconstantly are fledd
Away to London. But the man that's dead
Is gone unto a place more populous,
And tarries longer there, and waites for us.

An Epitaph on Sir John Walter, Lord Chiefe Baron

Farewell Example, Living Rule farewell;
Whose practise shew'd goodness was possible,
Who reach'd the full outstretch'd perfection
Of Man, of Lawyer, and of Christian.
    Suppose a Man more straight than Reason is,
Whose grounded Habit could not tread amisse
Though Reason slepd; a Man who still esteem'd
His wife his Bone; who still his children deem'd
His Limbes and future Selfe; Servants trayn'd friends;
Lov'd his Familiars for Themselves not ends:
Soe wise and Provident that dayes orepast
He ne're wish'd backe again; by whose forecast
Time's Locke, Time's Baldness, Future Time were one,
Since nought could mende nor marre one Action,
That man was he.
                Suppose an Advocate
In whose all-conquering tong true right was Fate;
That could not pleade among the grounded throng
Wrong Causes right nor rightfull causes wrong,
But made the burnish'd Truth to shine more bright
Than could the witnesses or Act in sight.
Who did soe breifely, soe perspicuously
Untie the knots of darke perplexity
That words appear'd like thoughts, and might derive
To dull Eares Knowledge most Intuitive.
    A judge soe weigh'd that Freinde and one of Us
Were heard like Titius and Sempronius.
All Eare, no Eie, no Hande; oft being par'd
The Eies Affections and the Hands Reward.
Whose Barre and Conscience were but two in Name,
Sentence and Closet-Censure still the Same:
That Advocate, that judge was He.

Suppose
A sound and settled Christian, not like those
That stand by fitts, but of that Sanctity
As by Repentance might scarce better'd be:
Whose Life was like his latest Houre, whose way
Outwent the Journey's Ende where others stay:
Who slighted not the Gospel for his Lawe,
But lov'd the Church more than the Bench, and sawe
That all his Righteousnes had yet neede fee
One Advocate beyond himselfe. 'Twas He.

    To this Good Man, Judge, Christian, now is given
Fair Memory, noe Judgment, and blest Heaven.

On the death of Sir Rowland Cotton Seconding that of Sir Robert

More Cottons yet? O let not envious Fate
Attempt the Ruine of our growing State.
O had it spar'd Sir Rowland, then might wee
Have almost spar'd Sir Robert's Library.
His life and th' others bookes taught but the same;
Death kils us twice in blotting twice one Name.
Give Him, and take those Reliques with consent;
Sir Rowland was a living monument.

To the Right Honourable the Lady Penelope Dowager of the late Vis-Count Bayning

Great Lady,

        Humble partners of like griefe
In bringing Comfort may deserve beliefe,
Because they Feele and Feyne not: Thus we say
Unto Ourselves, Lord Bayning, though away,
Is still of Christ-Church; somewhat out of sight,
As when he travel'd, or did bid good night,
And was not seen long after; now he stands
Remov'd in Worlds, as heretofore in Lands;
But is not lost. The spight of Death can never
Divide the Christian, though the Man it sever.

    The like we say to You: He's still at home,
Though out of reach; as in some upper roome,
Or Study: for His Place is very high,
His Thought is Vision; now most properly
Return'd he's Yours as sure, as e're hath been
The jewell in Your Cask, safe though unseen.

    You know that Friends have Eares as well as Eyes,
We hear Hee's well and Living, that well dies.

On the death of the Right Honourable the Lord Viscount Bayning

Though after Death, Thanks lessen into Praise,
And Worthies be not crown'd with gold, but bayes;
Shall we not thank? To praise Thee all agree;
We Debtors must out doe it, heartily.
Deserved Nobility of True Descent,
Though not so old in Thee grew Ancient:
We number not the Tree of Branched Birth,
But genealogie of Vertue, spreading forth
To many Births in value. Piety,
True Valour, Bounty, Meeknesse, Modesty,
These noble off-springs swell Thy Name as much,
As *Richards*, *Edwards*, three, foure, twenty such:
For in thy Person's linage surnam'd are
The great, the good, the wise, the just, the faire.
One of these stiles innobles a whole stemme;
If all be found in One, what race like him!
Long stayres of birth, unlesse they likewise grow
To higher vertue, must descend more low.
When water comes through numerous veins of lead,
'Tis water still; Thy blood, from One pipe's head,
Grew *Aqua-vitæ* streight, with spirits fill'd,
As not traduc'd, but rais'd, sublim'd, distill'd.
Nobility farre spread, I may behold,
Like the expanded skie, or dissolv'd gold,
Much rarified; I see't contracted here
Into a starre, the strength of all the spheare;
Extracted like the Elixir from the mine,
And highten'd so that 'tis too soone divine.
    Divinity continues not beneath;
Alas nor He; but though He passe by death,
He that for many liv'd, gaines many lives
After hee's dead: Each friend and servant strives

To give him breath in praise; this Hospital,
That Prison, Colledge, Church, must needs recall
To mind their Patron; whose rich legacies
In forreigne lands, and under other skies
To them assign'd, shew that his heart did even
In France love England, as in England Heaven:
Heav'n well perceiv'd this double pious love,
Both to his Country here, and that above:
Therefore the day, that saw Him landed here,
Hath seen him landed in his Haven there;
The selfe-same day (but two yeares interpos'd)
Saw Sun and Him round shining twice & clos'd.
     No Citizen so covetous could be
Of getting wealth, as of bestowing, He;
His Body and Estate went as they came,
Stript of Appendix Both, and left the same
But in th' Originall; Necessity
Devested one, the other Charity.
It cost him more to clothe his soule in death,
Than e're to cloth his flesh for short-liv'd breath;
And whereas Lawes exact from Niggards dead
A Portion for the Poore, they now are said
To moderate His Bounty; never such
Was known but once, that men should give too much:
A Tabernacle then was built, and now
The like in heav'n is purchased: Learn you how;
Partly by building Men, and partly by
Erecting walls, by new-found Chymistry,
Turning of Gold to Stones. Our Christ-Church Pile,
Great *Henrie's* Monument, shall grow awhile
With *Bayning's* Treasure; who a way hath took.
Like those at Westminster, to fill a nook
'Mongst beds of Kings. Thus speak, speak while we may
For Stones will speak when We are hush'd in Clay.

On the Death of the Ladie Caesar

Though Death to good men be the greatest boone,
I dare not think this Lady dyde so soone.
She should have livde for others: Poor mens want
Should make her stande, though she herselfe should faynt.
What though her vertuous deeds did make her seeme
Of equall age with old Methusalem?
She should have livde the more, and ere she fell
Have stretcht her little Span unto an Ell.
May wee not thinke her in a sleep or sowne,
Or that she only tries her bedde of ground?
Besides the life of Fame, is shee all deade?
As deade as Vertue, which together fledde:
As dead as men without it: and as cold
As Charity, that long ago grewe old.
Those eyes of pearle are under marble sett,
And now the Grave is made the Cabinett.
Tenne or an hundred doe not loose by this,
But all mankinde doth an Example misse.
A little earth cast upp betweene her sight
And us eclypseth all the world with night.
What ere Disease, to flatter greedy Death,
Hath stopt the organ of such harmlesse breath,
May it bee knowne by a more hatefull name
Then now the Plague: and for to quell the same
May all Physitians have an honest will:
May Pothecaries learne the Doctors skill:
May wandring Mountebanks, and which is worse
May an old womans medicine have the force
To vanquish it, and make it often flie,
Till destiny on's servant learne to die.
May death itselfe, and all its Armory
Bee overmatcht with one poore Recipe.
What need I curse it? for, ere Death will kill

Another such, so far estrang'd from ill,
So fayre, so kinde, so wisely temperate,
Time will cutt off the very life of Fate.
To make a perfect Lady was espyde
No want in her of anything but Pride:
And as for wantonnesse, her modesty
Was still as coole as now her ashes bee.
Seldome hath any Daughter lesse than her
Favourde the stampe of Eve her grandmother.
Her soule was like her body; both so cleare
As that a brighter eye than mans must peere
To find a Blott; nor can wee yet suspect
But only by her Death the least defect:
And were not that the wages due to Sinne
Wee might beleeve that spotlesse she had bin.

An Epitaph on Mr. Fishborne the great London benefactor, and his executor

What are thy gaines, O death, if one man ly
Stretch'd in a bed of clay, whose charity
Doth hereby get occasion to redeeme
Thousands out of the grave: though cold hee seeme
He keepes those warme that else would sue to thee,
Even thee, to ease them of theyr penury.
Sorrow I would, but cannot thinke him dead,
Whose parts are rather all distributed
To those that live; His pity lendeth eyes
Unto the blind, and to the cripple thighes,
Bones to the shatter'd corps, his hand doth make
Long armes for those that begg and cannot take:
All are supply'd with limbs, and to his freind
He leaves his heart, the selfe-same heart behind;
Scarce man and wife so much one flesh are found
As these one soule; the mutuall ty that bound
The first prefer'd in heav'n to pay on earth
Those happy fees which made them strive for death,
Made them both doners of each others store,
And each of them his own executor:
Those hearty summes are twice confer'd by either,
And yet so given as if confer'd by neither.
Lest some incroching governour might pare
Those almes and damne himselfe with poormens share,
Lameing once more the lame, and killing quite
Those halfe-dead carcases, by due foresight
His partner is become the hand to act
Their joynt decree, who else would fain have lackt
This longer date that so hee might avoyd
The praise wherewith good eares would not be cloy'd,
For praises taint our charity, and steale
From Heav'ns reward; this caus'd them to conceale

Theyr great intendment till the grave must needs
Both hide the Author and reveale the deeds.
His widdow-freind still lives to take the care
Of children left behind; Why is it rare
That they who never tied the marriage knott,
And but good deeds no issue ever gott,
Should have a troupe of children? All mankind
Beget them heyres, heyres by theyr freinds resign'd
Back into nature's keepeinge. Th' aged head
Turn'd creeping child of them is borne and bredd;
The prisons are theyr cradles where they hush
Those piercing cryes. When other parents blush
To see a crooked birth, by these the maim'd
Deform'd weake offcasts are sought out and claim'd
To rayse a Progeny: before on death
Thus they renew mens lives with double breath,
And whereas others gett but halfe a man
Theyr nobler art of generation can
Repayr the soule itselfe, and see that none
Bee cripled more in that then in a bone,
For which the Cleargy being hartned on
Weake soules are cured in theyr Physition,
Whose superannuat hatt or threadbare cloake
Now doth not make his words so vainly spoke
To people's laughter: this munificence
At once hath giv'n them ears, him eloquence.
Now Henryes sacriledge is found to bee
The ground that sets off Fishborne's charity,
Who from lay owners rescueing church lands,
Buys out the injury of wrongfull hands,
And shewes the blackness of the other's night
By lustre of his day that shines so bright.
    Sweet bee thy rest until in heav'n thou see
Those thankefull soules on earth preserv'd by thee,
Whose russet liv'ryes shall a Robe repay

That by reflex makes white the milky way.
Then shall those feeble limbs which as thine owne
Thou here didst cherish, then indeed bee known
To bee thy fellow limbs, all joyn'd in one;
For temples here renew'd the corner stone
Shall yeild thee thanks, when thou shall wonder at
The churches glory, but so poore of late,
Glad of thy almes! Because thy tender eare
Was never stop'd at cryes, it there shall heare
The Angells quire. In all things thou shalt see
Thy gifts were but religious Usury.

On the Death of Mr. James Van Otton

The first day of this month the last hath bin
To that deare soule. March never did come in
So lyonlike as now: our lives are made
As fickle as the weather or the shade.
March dust growes plenty now, while wasting fate
Strike heare to dust, well worth the proverbs rate.
I could be angry with the fates that they
This man of men so soone have stole away.
Meane they a kingdome to undoe, or make
The universe a Cripple while they take
From us so cheife a part, whose art knew how
To make a man a man, nor would allow
Nature an Heteroclite still to remaine
Irregular, but with a jugling paine
Deceive men of their greife, and make them know
That he could cure more than ere chance or foe
Dare to instring. Death now growes politique:
While Otton liv'd herselfe was weake and sicke
For want of food, therefore at him she aimde
Who bar'd her of her purpose. All is maimde,
All's out of joint, for in this fatall crosse
Behold Death's triumph and our fatall losse.

On Sir Thomas Savill dying of the small pox

Take, greedy death, a body here entomd
That by a thousand stroakes was made one wound,
Where all thy shafts were stuck with fatall ayme
Until a quiver this thy marke became,
Had Cæsar fifty wounds to let in thee
Because a troop of men might seem to bee
Comprised in that great Spirit, this had more
Whose deaths were equalld with the fruitfull store
Of hopeful vertues, though each wound did reach
The very heart, yet none could make a breach
Into his soule, a soule more fully drest
With vertuous gemmes than was his body prest
With hateful spots, and therefore every scarr
When death itselfe is dead shall be a starre.

Epitaph on Mr. Bridgeman

One pitt contains him now that could not dye
Before a thousand pitts in him did lye;
So many spotts upon his flesh were shewne
'Cause on his soule sinne fastned almost none.

To his Sister

Loving Sister: every line
Of your last letter was so fine
With the best mettle, that the grayne
Of Scrivener's pindust were but vayne:
The touch of Gold did sure instill
Some vertue more than did the Quill.
And since you write noe cleanly hand
Your token bids mee understand
Mine eyes have here a remedy
Wherby to reade more easily.
I doe but jest: your love alone
Is my interpretation:
My words I will recant, and sweare
I know your hand is wondrous faire.

A New Year's Gift

We are prevented; you whose Presence is
A Publick New-yeares gift, a Common bliss
To all that Love or Feare, give no man leave
To vie a Gift but first he shall receave;
Like as the Persian sun with golden Eies
First shines upon the Priest and Sacrifice.

     Ile on howere; May this yeare happier prove
Than all the Golden Age when Vertue strove
With nothing but with Vertue; may it bee
Such as the Dayes of Saturnes Infancy.
May every Tide and Season joyntly fitt
All your Intents and your Occasions hitt:
May every Grayne of Sand within your Glass
Number a fresh content before it pass.
And when success comes on, stand then each howre
Like Joshua's Day, & grow to three or fowre:
At last when this yeare rounds and wheeles away,
Bee still the next yeare like the old yeares Day.

To a Friend

Like to the hande which hath been usde to play
One lesson long, still runs the usuall way,
And waites not what the hearers bid it strike,
But doth presume by custome, this will like:
So runne my thoughts, which are so perfect growne,
So well acquainted with my passion,
That now they dare prevent mee with their hast,
And ere I thinke to sigh my sigh is past:
Tis past, and flowne to you, for you alone
Are all the object that I thinke upon,
And did not you supply my soule with thought
For want of action it to none were brought.
What though our absent armes may not enfold
Reall embraces, yet wee firmly hold
Each other in possession. Thus wee see
The Lord enjoy his Lands where ere hee bee.
If Kings possesst no more than where they sate
What were they greater than a mean estate?
This makes mee firmly yours, you firmly mine,
That somthing more than bodies us combine

A LETTER

Goe happy paper: by command
Take liberty to kisse her hand,
More white than any part of thee,
Although with spots thou graced bee.
The glory of the clearest day,
The morning ayre perfumed in May,
The first borne rose of all the Spring,
The down beneath a Turtle's wing,
A lute just reaching to the eare;
What ere is soft, or sweete, or fayre,
Are but her shreds, who fills the place
And some of every single grace.
As in a child the nurse descryes
The mother's lippes, the father's eyes,
The uncle's nose; and doth apply
An owner to each part; so I
In her could analyze the store
Of all the Choyce ere nature bore.
Each private peece to minde may call
Some worth; but none can match it all.
Poore emblems! they can but expresse
One element of comelinesse:
None are so rich to shew in one
All simples of perfection:
Nor can the Pencill represent
More than the outward lineament.
Then who can limbe the portrayture
Of beauties live behavior?
Or what can figure every kinde
Of Jewels that adorne her minde?
Thought cannot draw her picture full:
Even Thought to her is grosse and dull.

With Penne, Inke, and Paper to a distressed Friend

Here is paper, pen, and inke,
That your heart and seale may sinke
Into such markes as may expresse
A Soule much blest in heavinesse.

May your paper seeme as fayre
As yourselfe when you appeare:
May the Letters which you write
Look like black eye-lids on white.

May your penne such fancies bring
As one new puld from Cupid's wing:
That your paper, hand, and seale
His favour, heart, and Soule may steale.

Thanks for a Welcome

For your good lookes and your clarrett,
For oft bidding doe not spare it:
For tossing glasses to the toppe,
And after sucking off a droppe,
When scarce a droppe was left behinde,
Or that which nicknames wine, even winde:
For healthy mirth and lusty sherry
Such as made old Cato merry;
Such are our thanks that you may have
In blood the clarrett which you gave,
And in your service shall be spent
The spirits which your sacke hath lent.

A Paralell Between
Bowling and Preferment

Preferment, like a Game at bowles,
To feede our hope with diverse play
Heer quick it runnes, there soft it rowles:
The Betters make and shew the way.

As upper ground, so great Allies
Doe many cast on theyr desire:
Some uppe are thrust, and forc't to rise,
When those are stopt that would aspire.

Some whose heate and zeale exceed
Thrive well by Rubbs that curb theyr hast
Some that languish in their speede
Are cherisht by a gentle blast.

Some rest: and others cutting out
The same by whome themselves were made:
Some fetch a compasse farre about
And secretly the marke invade.

Some gett by knocke, and so advance
Theyr fortune by a boystrous ayme:
And some who have the sweetest chance
Theyr mistresse hitt, and winne the game.

The fayrest casts are those that owe
No thanks to Fortunes giddy sway:
Such honest men good bowles doe throw,
Whose owne true Byass cutts the way.

On a good legg and foot

If Hercules tall stature might bee guest
But by his thumbe, wherby to make the rest
In due proportion; the best rule that I
Would choose to measure Venus' beauty by
Should bee her legg and foot. If husbandmen
Measure theyr timber by the foot, why then
Not we our wives? Whether wee goe or stride
Those native compasses are seldome wide
Of telling true: the round and slender foot
Is a sure index, and a secrett note
Of hidden parts; and well this way may lead
Unto the closett of a maydenheade:
Here, Emblemes of our youth, we roses tye,
And here the garter, love's deare mystery:
For want of beauty here the peacock's pride
Letts fall her trayne, and fearing to bee spide
Shutts upp her paynted witnesses to lett
Those eyes from view which are but counterfett.
Who looks not if this part be good or evill
May meet with cloven feet and match the divell,
For this doth make the difference betweene
The more unhallowed creatures and the cleane,
Well may you judge her other stepps are lighte,
Her thoughts awry that doth not tread aright:
But then there's true perfection when wee see
Those parts more absolute that hidden bee:
Nature nere layd a fayre foundation
For an unworthy frame to rest upon.
Lett others view the topp and limbes throughout,
The deeper knowledge is to know the roote:
And reading of the face the weakest know,
What beauty is; the learned looke below;
Who, looking there, doe all the rest, descrie

As in a poole the moon we use to spie:
> Pardon (sweetehart) the pride of my desire
> If but to kisse your toe it should aspire.

ON JOHN DAWSON, BUTLER OF C.C.

Dawson the Butler's dead: Although I think
Poets were ne'er infusde with single drinke
Ile spend a farthing muse; some watry verse
Will serve the turne to cast upon his hearse;
If any cannot weepe amongst us here
Take off his pott, and so squeeze out a tear:
Weepe, O his cheeses, weepe till yee bee good,
Yee that are dry or in the sun have stood;
In mossy coats and rusty liveries mourne,
Untill like him to ashes you shall turne:
Weep, O ye barrells, lett your drippings fall
In trickling streams: make waste more prodigal
Than when our drinke is badde, that John may flote
To Styx in beere, and lift upp Charon's boate
With wholesome waves. And as our conduits run
With clarett at a Coronation,
So lett our channells flow with single tiffe,
For John, I hope, is crownde: take off your whiffe,
Yee men of Rosemary: Now drinke off all,
Remembring 'tis a Butler's funeral:
> Had he bin master of good double beere,
> My life for his, John Dawson had beene here.

JACKE-ON-BOTH-SIDES

I hold as fayth	What England's Church allows
What Rome's Church sayth	My conscience disavowes;
Where the King's head,	That Church can have no seame;
That flock's misled	That holdes the Pope supreme;
Where th' Altar's dressed	There's service scarce divine;
That People's blest	With table, bread and wine;
Who shuns the Masse	He's Catholique and wise;
He's but an Asse	Who the communion flyes;
Who Charity preach	That Church with schismes fraught;
They Heav'n soone reach	Where only fayth is taught;
On Faith t'rely,	No matter for good workes,
'Tis heresy	Makes Christians worse than Turkes.

The Chimney-Sweeper's Song

Hath Christmas furr'd your Chimneys,
    Or have the maides neglected,
Doe Fire-balls droppe from your Chimney's toppe,
    The Pidgin is respected,
Looke up with feare and horror,
    O how my mistresse wonders!
The streete doth crie, the newes doth fly,
    The boyes they thinke it thunders.

    Then up I rush with my pole and brush,
      I scour the chimney's Jacket,
    I make it shine as bright as mine,
      When I have rub'd and rak'd it.

Take heed, ten groates you'le forfeit,
    The Maior will not have under,
In vain is dung, so is your gun
    When brickes doe flie asunder:
Let not each faggot fright ye,
    When threepence will me call in,
The Bishopps foote is not worse than soote
    If ever it should fall in.

    Up will I rush, etc.

The sent, the smoake ne're hurts me,
    The dust is never minded,
Mine eyes are glasse men sweare as I passe
    Or else I had bin blinded,
For in the midst of Chimneys
    I laugh, I sing, I hollow,
I chant my layes in Vulcan's praise
    As merry as the swallow.

Still up I rush, etc.

With Engines and devices
    I scale the proudest chimney,
The Prince's throne to mine alone
    Gives place, the Starrs I climb ny.
I scorne all men beneath me
    While there I stand a scowring,
All they below looke like a Crow,
    Or men on Paules a tow'ring.

    Then down I rush, etc.

And as I downeward rumble
    What think you is my lott then?
A good neat's tongue in the inside hung,
    The maide hath it forgotten:
If e're the wanton mingled
    My inke with soote I wist not,
Howere the neate and harmless cheate
    Is worth a penny, is't not?

    Still doe I rush, etc.

Then cloth'd in soote and ashes
    I catch the maides that hast out,
Whos'ere I meete with smutt I greete,
    And pounse their lipps and wastcote:
But on the Sunday morning
    I looke not like a widgin,
Soe brave I stand with a point in my bande
    Men ask if I be Pidgin.

    Yet will I rush, etc.

Mulsacke I dare encounter
    For all his horne and feather,
Ile lay him a crown Ile roare him downe,
    I thinke heale ne'er come hether.
The Boyes that climbe like Crickets
    And steale my trade, Ile strippe them,
By priviledge I, growne Chimney hy,
    Soone out of towne will whippe them.

      Then will I rush, etc.

UPON THE SHERIFFS BEERE

The Sheriffe of Oxford late is grown so wise
As to reprieve his Beere till next assize:
Alas! twas not so quick, twas not so heady,
The Jury sate and found it dead already.

UPON A BUTCHER MARRYING
A TANNER'S DAUGHTER

A fitter match hath never bin—
The flesh is married to the skinne.

A Devonshire Song

Thou ne're wutt riddle, neighbour Jan
    Where Ich a late ha been-a?
Why ich ha been at Plymouth, Man,
    The leeke was yet ne're zeen-a
Zutch streetes, zutch men, zutch hugeous zeas,
    Zutch things with guns there tumbling
Thy zelfe leeke me thoudst blesse to see,
    Zutch overmonstrous grumbling

The towne orelaid with shindle stone
    Doth glissen like the skee-a:
Brave shopps stand ope, and all yeare long
    I thinke a Faire there bee-a:
A many gallant man there goth
    In gold that zaw the King-a;
The King zome zweare himzelfe was there,
    A man or zome zutch thing-a

Voole thou that hast noe water past,
    But thicka in the Moore-a,
To zee the zea would be agast,
    It doth zoe rage and roar-a:
Zoe zalt it tasts thy tongue will thinke
    The vier is in the water;
It is zoe wide noe lande is spide,
    Looke ne're zoe long thereafter

The Water vrom the Element
    None can dezeave cha vore-a,
It semmeth low, yet all consent
    Tis higher than the Moore-a
Tis strang how looking down the Cliffe
    Men looke mere upward rather;

If these same Eene had it not zeen
    Chud scarce beleeve my Vather

Amid the water woodden birds,
    And vlying houses zwimme-a,
All vull of goods as ich have heard
    And men up to the brimm-a:
They venter to another world
    Desiring to conquier-a,
Vor which their guns, vowle develish ons,
    Doe dunder and spitt vier-a.

Good neighbour Tom, how farre is that?
    This meazell towne chill leave-a ;
Chill mope noe longer here, that's vlatt
    To watch a Sheepe or Sheare-a:
Though it as varre as London be,
    Which ten mile ich imagin,
Chill thither hie for this place I
    Doe take in greate indudgin.

LOVE COMPARED TO A GAME OF TABLES

Love is a game at tables where the dye
Of mayds affections doth by fancie fly:
If once you catch their fancie in a blott
It's tenne to one if then you enter not:
You being a gamester then may boldly venter,
And if you finde the point lye open enter:
But marke them well, for by false playing then,
Doe what you can they will be bearing men.

Epitaphes on the monument
of Sir William Strode

Tread soft, for if you wake this Knight alone,
You raise an Hoast: Religions Champion,
His Cuntreys Staffe, Rights bold Distributer,
His Neighbours Guard, the Poor mans Almoner,
    Who dyes with Works about him, as did He,
    Shall rise attended thus triumphantly.

On His Lady Marie

Marie, incarnate Virtue, Soule and Skin
Both pure, whom Death not Life convincd of Sin,
Had Daughters like seven Pleiades; but She
Was a prime Star of greatest Claritie.

On His Lady Denys

Denys hath merited no slender praise,
In that She well supplied the Formers daies.
Conceive how Good she was, whose very worst
Unto her Knight was This, that She dyed First.

A Sonnet

Mourne, mourne, ye lovers: Flowers dying
Live againe, the cold defying,
But Beauties floure once dead dyes ever,
Falls as soone, and riseth never
Mourne, mourne, yee lovers: sadly singing
Love hath his Winter, and no springing.

A Sonnet

Sing aloud, harmonious sphears:
Let your concord reach Jove's eares
Play your old lessons ore againe,
And keepe time in every strayne,
For now the Gods are listning to your laies
As they are passing through the milky waies.

On his Mistresse

Gaze not on swans in whose soft breast
A full hatcht beauty seems to rest,
Nor a snow which falling from the sky
Hovers in its virginity.

Gaze not on roses though new blown
Grac'd with a fresh complexion,
Nor lily which no subtle bee
Hath rob'd by kissing chemistry.

Gaze not on that pure milky way
Where night vies splendour with the day,
Nor pearls whose silver walls confine
The riches of an Indian mine:

For if any emperesse appears
Swans moultring dy, snows melt to tears,
Roses do blush and hang their heads
Pale lillyes shrink into their beds;

The milky way rides poast to shrowd
It baffled glory in a clowd
And pearls do climb unto her eare
To hang themselves for envy there.

So have I seene stars big with light,
Proud lanthorns to the moone-ey'd night,
Which when Sol's rays were once display'd
Sunk in their sockets and decay'd

Upon a Gentlewoman's
Entertainment of him

Whether, sweet Mistress, I should most
Commend your music or your cost:
Your well-spread table, or the choise
Banquet of your hand and voyce,
There's none will doubt: for can there be
'Twixt earth and heaven analogy?
Or shall a trencher or dish stand
In competition with your hand?
Your hand that turns men all to ear,
Your hand whose every joints a sphere:
For certainly he that shall see
The swiftnesse of your harmony,
Will streightwayes in amazement prove
The spheares to you but slowly move;
And in that thought confess that thus
The Heavens are come down to us,
As he may well, when he shall hear
Such airs as may be sung even there:
Your sacred Anthems, strains that may
Grace the eternal Quire to play:
And certainly they were prepar'd
By Angels only to be heard.
Then happy I that was so blest
To be yours and your music's guest,
For which I'd change all other cheer,
Thinking the best, though given, too dear.
For yours are delicates that fill,
And filling leave us empty still:
Sweetmeats that surfeit to delight,
Whose fullness is mere appetite.
Then farewell all our heavenly fare,
Those singing dainties of the air,

For you to me do seem as good
As all the consorts of the wood;
And might I but enjoy by choice,
My Quire should be your only voice.

NOTES TO THE POEMS

The source for these texts is the 1907 edition of the *Poetical Works of William Strode*, edited and published by Bertram Dobell in London.

Another Version, to his Mistresse (p.14)
The text is taken from the miscellany *Parnassus Biceps*. It is printed there as two distinct poems, the second of which is attributed to Thomas Carew (1594–1640), and starts with the line, 'In those faire cheeks two pitts doe lye'. Standard editions of Carew's poems include this poem as one of his.

Basilisks — the basilisk was reputed to be King of the snakes, with the ability to kill with a single glance.

Song: On a Sigh (p.16)
3rd Stanza, Line 3: *Æolus* — ruler of the winds.

Song: On the Baths (p.18)
The reference is to the city of Bath.

Bladud — a legendary early King of the Britons, first listed by Geoffrey of Monmouth in his *History of the Kings of Britain*. In some accounts, Bladud was founder of the city of Bath.

Song: A strange gentlewoman passing by his window (p.21)
Pygmalion: In Ovid's *Metamorphoses*, a Cypriot sculptor who fell in love with his own sculpture of a woman.

A Translation of The Nightingale out of Strada (p.25)
from Famiamus Strada's Latin volume *Prolusiones Academicae, Oratoriae, Historicae, Poeticae* (1617). The fable of the musical duel between a lutenist and a nightingale was written in imitation of Claudian (late 4th/early 5th century AD).

On Westwell Downes (p.28)
There is a Westwell Downs in Kent, but there is also a lesser-known Westwell in Oxfordshire and to this day there is a Downs Farm there. Given Strode's residence in Oxford, it may be safe to assume that he refers to the Oxfordshire Westwell.

On a great hollow Tree (p.30)

Jacke Maypole — the maypole, around which revellers danced on the May-day festival.

Monychus — a centaur, mentioned by Ovid in the *Metamorphoses*, Book 12. Also a generic term for centaurs.

Ceres' oake — an ancient oak in a grove sacred to Ceres, chopped down by order of Erysichthon. When struck by an axe, the oak bled. Despite the cries of the wood-nymph who dwelt within the tree, Erysichthon still chopped it down. He was cursed with eternal hunger by Ceres.

Erisichthon — Erysichthon.

Silenus — (also Seilenos); Greek god of drunkenness.

Minerva — Roman goddess of warriors and poetry, and the inventor of music. The daughter of Jupiter.

Argos — city in the Peleponnese, Greece.

Delphos — Delphi, home of the most famous of the ancient Greek oracles.

Dodona forest — a grove which was the site of an ancient Greek oracle.

Hamadryades — wood nymphs, who inhabited specific trees. According to legend, a hamadryad would die if her tree died.

citterns — the cittern was an early form of the guitar, and was related to the lute. It was an instrument familiar to all in Strode's period.

On Fayrford Windowes (p.33)

Fairford is in the Gloucestershire Cotswolds. The parish church of St. Mary is renowned for its medieval stained-glass windows.

two turtles in one cage: here, and elsewhere in this collection, *turtle* refers to the turtledove.

Momus Wish: Dobell explains as follows: "The reference is to Lucian's Hermotimus, ch. 20, where Momus, the personification of fault-finding, has to decide a contesty in skill between Athena, who has made a horse, Poseidon, who made a bull, and Hephaestus, who has made a man. He criticised Hephaestus severely 'because he had not made windows in the man's breast, that by opening these anybody could see clearly his wishes or thoughts, and his truth or untruth.'"

On a Gentlewoman's blistred lipp (p.36)
Line 8: *seize* — read as 'size'.

On a Gentlewoman's Watch ... (p.43)
ell: a unit of measure, usually 45 inches in its English form. Used
  mainly in tailoring.

On a Gentlewoman walking in the snowe (p.46)
Cloris / Chloris: a name used frequently in pastoral poems for an
  idealised female character.

A Superscription ... (p.47)
Arcadia: a pastoral work in prose and verse by Sir Philip Sidney,
  written 1580, and published in 1590 in Sidney's revised, but
  incomplete, second version. Another version, splicing part
  of the unpublished first version with this 1590 edition, was
  published by Sidney's sister in 1593. An enormously influential
  work.
Philoclea: character in *Arcadia*, a cover-name for Sidney's own love,
  Lady Penelope Devereaux.
Pamela: the main female character in *Arcadia*.

On Death & Resurrection (p.52)
Ahaz: King of Judah in the 8th century BC, whose reign is covered
  in Kings, Isaiah and Chronicles. An idolatrous King who
  nonetheless saved Jerusalem from its enemies by paying tribute
  to the Assyrian King Tiglath-Pileser, who in turn destroyed
  those who threatened his new vassal.

On the Life of Man (p.56)
This poem has no certain attribution, and has been assigned in the
  past to Sir Walter Raleigh, among others. It should be noted
  that, after Raleigh's execution, a great number of poems were
  attributed to him that were in fact by others.

On the Death of Mistresse Mary Prideaux (p.57)
Mary Prideaux was the daughter of Dr. John Prideaux (1578–1650),
later Bishop of Worcester.

On the Death of Dr. Lancton (p.66)

William Langton was President of Magdalen College, Oxford, 1610–1626.

An Epitaph on Sir John Walter, Lord Chiefe Baron (p.70).

Titius and Sempronius: There are several possible candidates for 'Sempronius' but the most likely, given the context, is Publius Sempronius Gracchus, a first-century AD Roman senator who sponsored land reform, to benefit poor farmers. He was assassinated by his political enemies. 'Titius' is likely to be Marcus Titius, suffect consul in 31 BC (i.e. awarded the post on the death of the previous incumbent), a sometime supporter of Mark Antony and Cleopatra who later switched sides to follow Octavian, and became Governor of Syria in the early Empire.

On the Death of the Ladie Caesar (p.75)

Née Ann Hungate, the second Lady Caesar, wife to Sir Julius Caesar (1580–1636), and niece of Francis Bacon.

An Epitaph on Mr Fishborne ... (p.77)

Richard Fishborne (or Fishburne) was a wealthy cloth merchant who died in 1625, leaving a large proportion of his wealth for the benefit of the poor.

The Chimney-Sweeper's Song (p.91)

Mulsacke (sometimes also Mulled-Sacke) was a famous chimney-sweep of the era, and is referred to in other poems and plays of the period.

On his Mistresse (p.98)

Ascribed to Henry Noel in Henry Lawes' *Ayres and Dialogues*. Dobell also refers to a manuscript where it is headed 'Dr. Love on his Mistresse'. Dobell included it in his own Strode collection because of its quality, and also because of a previous (albeit insecure) attribution to Strode. I would concur with Dobell's high estimation of the poem, and thus follow his lead here.

www.ingramcontent.com/pod-product-compliance
Lightning Source LLC
Chambersburg PA
CBHW022157080426

42734CB00006B/473